D0848846

Action Sports

Surfing

Bill Gutman

Illustrated with photographs
by Shawn Frederick

Reading consultant:
John Manning, Professor of Reading
University of Minnesota

Capstone Press
MINNEAPOLIS

Copyright © 1995 Capstone Press. All rights reserved. No part of this book may be reproduced in any form without written permission from the publisher.

Printed in the United States of America.

Capstone Press • 2440 Fernbrook Lane • Minneapolis, MN 55447

Editorial Director   John Coughlan
Managing Editor   John Martin
Copy Editor   Gil Chandler

Library of Congress Cataloging-in-Publication Data

Gutman, Bill.
  Surfing / by Bill Gutman.
    p. cm.-- (Action sports)
  Includes bibliographical references and index.
  ISBN 1-56065-235-7
  1. Surfing--Juvenile literature. [1.Surfing.]   I. Title.
II. Series.
GV840.S8G88 1995
729.3'2--dc20   94-28047
                                                     CIP
                                                     AC

ISBN: 1-56065-235-7

99 98 97 96 95   8 7 6 5 4 3 2 1

Table of Contents

Chapter 1   A Look at Surfing 5

Chapter 2   A Look at the Past 9

Chapter 3   The Equipment 15

Chapter 4   Getting Started 21

Chapter 5   Basic Maneuvers 29

Chapter 6   Surfing Safety 37

Important Surfing Areas 42

Wave Pools 43

Glossary 44

To Learn More 46

Index 48

Chapter 1
A Look at Surfing

The sport of surfing is one of the most healthful and exciting in the world. Top surfers ride high waves that move at speeds up to 35 miles (56 kilometers) per hour. Wind and spray blow around them as they skillfully balance on their colorful boards.

Finding the Perfect Wave

Sun, wind, water, sandy beaches, and deep blue skies are all a part of the surfing scene. Many surfers like to travel around the world in search of natural beauty. Others say they are looking for the perfect wave, and that part of the fun is trying to find it.

Starting Out Slowly

Surfing also takes a great deal of skill to master. The beginner cannot just go out and try to catch a huge wave. He or she could get hurt or even drown.

As with other sports, the new surfer must start slowly. First of all, the beginner must be a good swimmer. Learning how to get up on the surfboard–and stay up–is the next step. Once a surfer is riding a wave, he or she has to know just what the wave will do. All this takes time and practice.

The result is well worth it. Most surfers love their sport and continue to ride the waves for many, many years. Once you start, chances are you will surf forever.

Surfers need a lot of practice to learn how to ride the big waves.

Chapter 2

A Look at the Past

The sport of surfing goes back many hundreds of years. No one really knows exactly when or where it began. Most think **"wave sliding"** started off the islands of the Pacific Ocean. The islanders learned to enjoy the high surf. Some cruised over the waves in canoes. Others swam through them. Still others used large wooden boards to ride them.

Already a Sport

When Captain James Cook reached Hawaii in 1778, he found that surfing was already a popular sport. The Hawaiians used very heavy

The first surfboards were very long. Today surfers use both "longboards" and "shortboards."

boards that were up to 18 feet (5.5 meters) long. They held contests and gave prizes to the winners.

Surfing in the United States

It would take more than a hundred years before surfing spread to the mainland of the

United States. A man named George Freeth brought surfing from Hawaii to Redondo Beach, California, in 1908. Soon the new sport was attracting surfers to the California beaches. But not many people could handle the huge boards the Hawaiians used.

A New Board

The sport did not really take hold until the early 1950s. That's when a young man named Bob Simmons changed surfing forever. Simmons felt there was a better way to surf than riding 120-pound (54-kilogram) boards. So he built another kind of board.

The board Simmons built was made of balsa wood, the world's lightest wood. Simmons' new board had a fin that pointed down from the tail end. The fin made it easier to control the board and turn in the surf. The new design also made it easy for surfers to cut and shape the boards the way they wanted. Soon surfers were popping up all along the California coast.

An Even Better Board

By 1956 some boards were being made of plastic foam, which was even lighter than balsa wood. This started the first real boom in surfing. With the older, heavy boards, riders almost always rode straight to shore. With the lighter boards they could do many more things.

A New Style of Surfing

Surfers using these new boards quickly learned how to ride across the face of a wave. They could also move up to the **nose**, or front, of the board and do all kinds of tricks and maneuvers. A **radical** new style of surfing had begun. Surfing was here to stay.

The tremendous power of a breaking wave can test the strength and skill of even the best surfers.

Chapter 3
The Equipment

Many years of practice and experimentation have gone into the making of today's surfboards.

Most surfboards are now made from a lightweight foam covered with fiberglass. Board makers glue two pieces of foam together with a one-eighth to one-quarter inch (.3 to .6 centimeter) layer of balsa wood between them. This balsa **stringer** gives the board its strength.

Types of Boards

The fiberglass covering is measured in ounces. A four-ounce (113-gram) covering, the thinnest and lightest, is used mainly by racers. Most recreational surfers use boards wrapped with six-ounce (170-gram) fiberglass. The best board for a beginner is a board covered with eight-ounce (226-gram) fiberglass. It's a heavier, more durable board. It's also more stable and easier to use.

Longboards and Shortboards

Back in the 1960s, most surfers used **longboards.** Most of these boards were from 9 to 11 feet (2.7 to 3.3 meters) long and weighed at least 25 pounds (11.3 kilograms). In the early 1970s, the boards got shorter and lighter. By the 1980s, most surfers were using **shortboards**. Shortboards range from about 5 feet 10 inches to 6 feet 4 inches (1.8 to 1.9 meters) long. They are easier to turn and control than longboards. Most surfers use shortboards for tricks and fancy moves. **Hot-doggers** also use shortboards because of the way they can spin and turn through the waves.

The three fins under the rear of a surfboard were developed in the late 1970s by Simon Anderson.

The Fins

Modern boards, short or long, have three fins or **skegs** underneath. Simon Anderson, an Australian, developed the three-fin design in the late 1970s. He called the three-fin boards "thrusters." Two of the fins are on the edge, or

rails, with one on each side. The third is in the
middle and slightly to the rear, at the tail of the
board.

The Comeback of the Longboard
In the 1990s, the longboard has made a
comeback. Modern longboards are from 7 feet
6 inches to 9 feet 6 inches (2.3 meters to 2.9
meters) long. They are now the board of
choice for surfers who ride the waves for pure
enjoyment. These longboarders aren't
interested in hot-dogging or doing tricks. They
just want to enjoy the surf, the sun, and the
beauty of the outdoors.

The new longboards have kept many of the
shortboard's qualities. The three-fin design
gives today's longboarder more control and
stability.

Find the Right Board
Experienced surfers can try out different
designs until they find a board they really like.
Beginners should start with a mid-length board.
A seven-foot (two-meter) board is a good size

for a newcomer. It will have more buoyancy, which means it will float better and support more weight than a smaller board. Buoyant boards are the easiest to paddle into the surf and the best for learning the basics of surfing.

Waxing

All surfers wax their boards. A good surfboard wax helps to protect the board from the salt water. It also gives the rider a better grip on the board. A waxed board isn't as slippery as an unwaxed one. Be sure to put on wax with a back-and-forth motion. Don't rub it on with a circular motion.

Some surfers also use a special tape on the board to give their feet a better grip.

Chapter 4
Getting Started

The first thing a beginning surfer must know is how to swim. This might sound silly to some people. They might think that because surfing is done so close to shore, surfers don't have to swim well or even swim at all. This is not true!

A surfer has to deal with large and powerful waves. Big waves can throw surfers from their boards. Once in the water, the surfer must keep control while waves toss him about and break over him. So before you surf, make sure you can swim, and swim well.

One spot for a good ride is atop the wave's crest, just as it breaks on the shore.

Buying a Board

Next, get a board. If you don't have one, you can borrow one from a friend or rent one. Then, if you like the sport and want to continue, you can buy your own board. Good surfboards can be costly, so make sure you enjoy surfing before you spend your money.

At the Beach

For your first ride, you should pick a beach where small, smooth waves are breaking on the shore. Check for large rocks or other obstacles in the water. Also, make sure there aren't a lot of swimmers or waders in the area. It's a good idea to have a buddy with you—a surfer can be hit by his own board, or collide with someone and need help.

Paddling

If you know how to swim and have a board, it's time to paddle out. Practice paddling your board through calm water first. Lie straight down on the center of the board to keep it stable. A larger board will have more buoyancy and be easier to paddle. If you start with a short and light board, you will have a hard time paddling.

Once on the board, you should paddle with both arms. As you reach forward, put your hand into the water, then your wrist, and finally your arm up to your elbow.

Pull both arms along the side of the board. At the end of each stroke, lift your arms out, bring them forward, and start the stroke again. A strong paddler will get more speed and stability on the board.

Turning

The beginner should also practice making turns by paddling backward with one hand and forward with the other. The board will turn towards the arm that's paddling backward. Beginners should master the turns before they get up to ride. After learning the basics, you can begin paddling out straight through the waves.

The next step is to ride several small waves while lying on your stomach. This will show you how the board moves on a wave and what it's like to have the wave break over you. After doing this a number of times, you should be ready to stand up on your board.

This surfer may have some trouble staying up on the board after going airborne.

"Catching" the Wave

Surfers can ride on two different parts of the wave. The first is the smooth part, or **wall**, of a wave that has not yet broken. The other is the white water or **"soup"** that appears after a wave breaks. Experienced surfers always want to ride the unbroken wall.

Beginners should start by trying to ride the white water, which is easier to catch. Catching a wave takes practice!

A big wave can surround a surfer who's able to catch the wave just right.

Once you have paddled out to where the waves start breaking, turn your board around and wait for a wave. When it's about 10 to 15 feet (3 to 4.5 meters) behind you, begin paddling hard toward shore. When the wave catches and begins lifting the board, it's time to stand up. This is done by pushing up your

BISMARCK-HENNING
GRADE SCHOOL
LIBRARY

body with both arms. At the same time, drag your knees forward.

The Kneeling Stance

Now sit back on your haunches so you're kneeling in the center of the board and slightly to the rear of the mid-point. Ride a few times in this kneeling position to learn how shifting your weight can turn the board.

By leaning to the left and slightly to the rear, you will turn the board left. It will turn right when you lean right. Leaning back will slow the board. Lean forward slightly, and it will go faster. After doing this a few times, you're ready to stand up.

Standing Up

To stand up, you can almost skip the kneeling position. In one quick motion, push up with your arms and drag your knees forward. With a hop, your feet should hit the board, one in front of the other. Then you can rise from your squatting position.

Congratulations. You're surfing!

BISMARCK PUBLIC SCHOOLS
GRADE SCHOOL
LIBRARY

Chapter 5
Basic Maneuvers

The first thing to try once you're up on the board is the basic stance. Beginners must get this stance right or they will wipe out before they get started. It doesn't matter which foot is forward. Most surfers like to stand with their left foot forward. Those who put their right foot forward are using a **goofy-foot** stance.

The Basic Stance
In the basic stance, both feet point to the sides, at almost a right angle to the front of the board. The feet should be about shoulder-

Leaning on the balls of the feet and shifting forward will steer the board to the right.

width apart and placed in the middle of the board, directly over the center line.

Bending slightly at the knees will help your balance. You can also widen your stance somewhat for more stability. Do not lock your front knee out of fear of falling forward. Relaxing your body will give you better balance and control.

Start with your arms held away from the body, but not too high. Shifting your arms will help you control the board.

Turning

As soon as a new surfer learns how to stand on the board and ride a wave, he or she has to learn how to turn. If a rider can't turn, the board will just slide down the front of the wave and nose into the water. So turning is very important for every surfer.

The Leaning Turn

The best turn for the beginner is the leaning turn. It is done by shifting your weight, not by moving your feet. While the feet stay in the basic riding position, the board is turned to the right or left by leaning. At the same time, the surfer shifts his or her weight to the balls of the feet or to the heels.

To turn left from the basic stance, shift your weight to the heels and lean slightly backward. To keep your balance, extend both arms out in front of you. As you do this, the board will

gradually turn. To turn right, shift your weight forward to the balls of your feet. This time, move both arms back and to the rear. Practice right and left turns on small waves.

The Rear Foot Turn

Another basic turn is the rear foot turn. To turn left, the rear foot is moved slightly back and toward the left side of the board. From a basic stance (left foot forward), that means the right foot is moved back.

From the goofy-foot stance (right foot forward), the left foot would be moved back and then toward the left side of the board. A right turn is made the opposite way–by moving the rear foot back toward the right side.

As you move the rear foot, shift your weight to the front foot. The rear foot turn involves shifting the weight from foot to foot, while the leaning turn involves shifting the weight between the balls and heels of the feet.

Beginners may have trouble keeping their balance when they first use the rear foot turn. But they will soon get used to it. Most good surfers use both kinds of turns. After awhile, both will come naturally. You'll find yourself turning your board without even thinking about it.

Trimming

There is one more basic maneuver that all new surfers have to know. It's called **trimming** the board or just trimming. After each turn, the surfer must bring the board back to "trim." That means moving the board so that it's lying flat along the surface of the water.

When the board is in trim there will be a trail of water coming from both sides of the nose. As much of the board as possible will be in contact with the face of the wave. A board in trim gives the surfer speed, power, and control.

Trimming is done by shifting the weight from the front to the rear foot, or from the rear to the front foot. It takes practice and a good feel for the board.

Sometimes, if your feet are too close together, it's difficult to trim with just a weight shift. The surfer should move the front foot closer to the nose or the rear foot closer to the tail before shifting his weight. This wider stance will make it easier to trim correctly.

By practicing these basic techniques, new surfers will quickly get better at catching and riding the waves.

Chapter 6
Surfing Safety

1. Know How to Swim.

The first rule of safe surfing was mentioned earlier. Make sure you're a strong swimmer before you start riding waves. There is no way around this rule. If you can't swim, don't surf. If you're a weak swimmer, become a strong one. Remember, you can be thrown off your board while catching a wave. If the board is swept away, you'll have to swim to shore in the pounding surf.

2. Never Surf Alone.

Another important rule of safety: never surf alone! Make sure there is someone around to help you if you get in trouble. Surfers can sometimes be hit and knocked out by their own boards. If they don't get help, they drown. Also, don't surf around a crowd of other surfers. Heavy traffic on the waves can lead to trouble.

3. Quit When You're Tired.

Surfing is a very tiring sport. A new surfer can quickly get worn out. Make sure you're physically fit before you start. Don't keep surfing when you're tired or when your muscles ache. A tired surfer is much more likely to have an accident.

4. Watch Out for the Board.

Another danger is the loose board. After a **wipeout**, the surfboard can fly around like a heavy club. Boards have knocked out even top surfers. Some have even drowned after being hit by a loose board.

5. Try to Avoid a Wipeout.

There are some ways to avoid a dangerous
wipeout. Don't tackle waves you aren't ready
for. If you don't have the skill, stay away from
the big ones. When you are on a big wave, try
to avoid wiping out. Don't think it's fun to be
pitched off the board. If you lose your balance,
keep in contact with the board as long as
possible. In small and medium-size waves,
you may be able to hold on as you fall.

6. Know the Best Way to Fall

If you start to fall and can't hold on to the board, there are some basic rules to follow. It's much safer to fall off the back of the board than the front. If you can't fall off the back, fall to the side.

It's also safer to fall feet first and, when you hit the water, roll up into a ball. By doing this, you will sink quickly. Your arms and legs will be saved from injury. Your arms will also protect your head. If you have to wipe out, try to relax as you fall. Too much struggling will make you tired.

7. Know Your Skill Level

You'll see many surfers doing tricks. "Hot-dogging" is a big part of surfing. Many surfers have practiced their moves for years. But some tricks can be dangerous. Never try them until you're a very skilled surfer. Then go slowly. Let someone who knows how to do these tricks teach you. Watch and learn. Don't try more than you can do safely.

8. Know the Surfing Area

You should also learn all about the sea and surf. Talk to veteran surfers. Ask questions. Learn about waves, the coastal environment, currents, undertows, and riptides. Know where you're surfing. Know what the bottom is like. Is it just sand? Or does it have rocks and sharp coral below the surface?

9. Be Your Best

Maybe the best rule is one that applies to all sports. Become the best surfer you can be. Learn as much about the sport as you can. And always think of safety first.

Important Surfing Areas

California: Hermosa Beach, Huntington Beach, Malibu, Newport Beach, Rancho Palos Verdes, Santa Cruz, San Clemente, Seal Beach

Florida: Sebastian Inlet

Hawaii: Banzai Pipeline, Halaiewa, Sunset Beach, Waimea, Waikiki

New York: Montauk Point, Long Island

North Carolina: Cape Hatteras

Virginia: Virginia Beach

New Jersey: Atlantic City

Rhode Island: Middletown

Surfing Areas around the World

Australia: Kirra Point, Queensland; Perth; Sydney; Torquay (near Melbourne)

Brazil: Bara de Juca

England: Newquay and St. Ives, Cornwall

France: Biarritz

Mexico: Baja California

Wave Pools

Wave pools give landlocked people a chance to enjoy surfing. Some of the pools listed here may permit surfing only at special times. Be sure to check.

Arizona: Tempe, Island of Big Surf

California: Irvine, Wild Rivers Water Park

Florida: Lake Buena Vista, Typhoon Lagoon, Walt Disney World

Pennsylvania: Allentown, Wildwater Kingdom

Texas: New Braunfels, Schlitterbahn Water Park

Alberta, Canada: West Edmonton, West Edmonton Mall

Glossary

crest–the top of a wave just before it breaks

deck–the top portion of the surfboard

drop in–the act of sliding down the face of a wave right after catching it

goofy-foot–placing the right foot forward in the basic riding stance

hot-dogging–doing showy, eye-catching, and difficult moves on the board

longboards–surfboards that are from 84 inches (213 centimeters) to 132 inches (335 centimeters) in length

nose–the front end of the surfboard

radical–popular term for anything extreme, from the shape of the surfboard to difficult maneuvers on the board

rail–the edge of a surfboard

shortboards–surfboards that are about 72 inches (183 centimeters) long and are easier to maneuver than longer boards

skegs–the fins on the underside of a surfboard

soup–a mixture of air bubbles and churning water that gives a breaking wave its white water look

stringer–a narrow layer of balsa wood that adds strength to the foam that makes up a surfboard

tail–the rear portion of the surfboard

trimming–to put the board flat on the surface of the water

wave sliding–an old term that describes surfing done by Pacific Islanders for hundreds of years.

wall–the smooth part of a wave

wipeout–a sudden or bad fall from the surfboard

To Learn More

Holden, Phil. *Wind and Surf.* Minneapolis, MN: Lerner Publications, 1992.

Werner, Doug. *Surfer's Start-Up: A Beginner's Guide to Surfing.* Ventura, CA: Pathfinder, 1993.

Magazines:

Surfer magazine
P.O. Box 1028
Dana Point, CA 92629.

Surfing Magazine
P.O. Box 3010
San Clemente, CA 92025

Longboard Quarterly
110 East Palizada Suite 301
San Clemente, CA 92672

Videos:

Session Impossible. Surf and Skate Video Network, 1991.

The Legends of Malibu. Frontline Video, 1987.

Some Useful Addresses

National Scholastic Surfing Association
P.O. Box 495
Huntington Beach, CA 92648

Surfrider Foundation
P.O. Box 2704
Huntington Beach, CA 92647

U.S. Surfing Federation
7104 Island Village Drive
Long Beach, CA 90803

Acknowledgments

Capstone Press thanks Bob Pace, president of the U.S. Surfing Federation; and Nick Carroll, editor of *Surfing Magazine*.

Index

Anderson, Simon, 17
Australia, 17, 42

balsa wood, 11-12, 15
beginners, 7, 16, 18, 21-27, 29-31, 34-35
buoyancy, 19

California, 11, 42, 43
canoes, 9
Cook, Captain James, 9
currents, 41

falling, 40
fiberglass, 15-16
fins, 11, 17-18
foam, 12, 15
Freeth, George, 11

goofy-foot, 29, 33

Hawaii, 9, 42
Hawaiians, 9, 11
hot-dogging, 16, 18, 40

longboards, 16, 18
loose boards, 38

obstacles, 23
Pacific Ocean, 9
paddling, 19, 23-24, 26

rear-foot turn, 33-34
Redondo Beach, 11
riptides, 41

safety, 23, 37-41
shortboards, 16
Simmons, Bob, 11
soup, 25
stances, 26-27; basic stance, 29-32; goofy-foot stance, 29-33
stringer, 15
swimming, 7, 21, 23

traffic, 38
trimming, 34-35
turning, 24, 27, 31-34

undertows, 41

"wave sliding," 9
wax, 19
wind, 5